D1408465

Day and Night

by Henry Pluckrose

Gareth Stevens Publishing
A WORLD ALMANAC EDUCATION GROUP COMPANY

Please visit our web site at: **www.garethstevens.com**
For a free color catalog describing Gareth Stevens' list of high-quality books
and multimedia programs, call 1-800-542-2595 (USA) or 1-800-461-9120 (Canada).
Gareth Stevens Publishing's Fax: (414) 332-3567.

Library of Congress Cataloging-in-Publication Data

Pluckrose, Henry Arthur.
    Day and night / by Henry Pluckrose. — North American ed.
      p. cm. — (Let's explore)
    Includes bibliographical references and index.
    ISBN 0-8368-2958-1 (lib. bdg.)
    1. Earth—Rotation—Juvenile literature. 2. Day—Juvenile literature.
    3. Night—Juvenile literature. [1. Earth—Rotation. 2. Day. 3. Night.]
    I. Title.
    QB633.P58   2001
    525'.35—dc21   2001031110

This North American edition first published in 2001 by
Gareth Stevens Publishing
A World Almanac Education Group Company
330 West Olive Street, Suite 100
Milwaukee, WI 53212 USA

This U.S. edition © 2001 by Gareth Stevens, Inc. Original edition © 2000 by Franklin Watts.
First published in 2000 by Franklin Watts, 96 Leonard Street, London, EC2A 4XD, United
Kingdom. Additional end matter © 2001 by Gareth Stevens, Inc.

Series editor: Louise John
Series designer: Jason Anscomb
Gareth Stevens editor: Monica Rausch
Gareth Stevens designer: Katherine A. Kroll

Picture credits: Ray Moller Photography cover and p. 31; Science Photo Library pp. 4
(Chris Butler), 11 (Geoff Tompkinson); Robert Harding pp. 6 (Roy Rainford), 9 (Nigel Francis),
23 (A. Woolfitt), 15 (Roy Rainford); Bruce Coleman pp. 16 (Kim Taylor), 18 (Astrofoto), 13
(Uwe Walz), 28 (George McCarthy); Eye Ubiquitous p. 21 (James Davis Travel Photography);
Oxford Scientific Films p. 24 (Edward Parker); © M. Douglas/The Image Works p. 27.

Printed in the United States of America

1 2 3 4 5 6 7 8 9 05 04 03 02 01

Contents

Earth's Axis 4

Daytime 6

Nighttime 8

Sunrise 10

Sunset 12

Electric Lights 14

The Moon 16

Stars 18

Summer Days 20

Winter Nights 22

Working during the Day 24

Working at Night 26

Nocturnal Animals 28

Sleeping 30

Index / More Books to Read 32

Imagine a long stick running straight through the center of Earth, from the North Pole to the South Pole. This imaginary stick is called Earth's axis. Earth turns on its axis. As Earth turns, the Sun shines on it, sending heat and light.

During a day, one part of Earth faces the Sun, while another part of Earth faces away from the Sun. When the part of Earth where you are is facing the Sun, it is daytime.

When the part of Earth where you are is facing away from the Sun, it is nighttime. It is dark at night, when the Sun is not shining on Earth.

Daytime begins when we see the Sun rise in the sky. We use the words *sunrise*, *daybreak*, and *dawn* to describe this time of day.

Daytime ends when the Sun sets and we can no longer see it. *Nightfall* and *sunset* are words we use to describe this time of day.

As daylight fades, we turn on electric lights to help us see. At night, lights shining on buildings and statues can make them look beautiful.

The Moon also shines at night. But the Moon does not shine its own light. Instead, the Moon reflects light from the Sun.

At night, we can see many stars, too. Unlike the Moon, stars make their own light. We cannot see stars during the day because the Sun's light is too bright.

In summer, daytime lasts longer than night. Midsummer Day is the longest day of the year. In some countries, such as Finland and Sweden, people celebrate this day with dancing and festivals. Some people dance around a maypole, a pole decorated with flowers or ribbons.

In winter, nights are longer than days. People celebrate in winter, too. Can you think of one special holiday we celebrate in winter?

Most people work during the day. It is much easier for this farmer to care for his animals in the daytime, when the Sun is shining.

Some people have to work at night. This snowplow driver clears the roads at night so they will be safe for people to drive on when daylight comes. Can you think of other people who work through the night?

Some animals sleep during the day and stay awake at night. We say these animals are "nocturnal." Owls are nocturnal animals. They hunt at night. Their large eyes help them see mice in the dark.

Most people sleep through the night. They rest and dream until another day begins. Sweet dreams!

Index

animals 25, 29

axis 5

buildings 14

day 7, 10, 12, 14, 19,
   20, 22, 25, 26, 29, 30

Earth 5, 7, 8

electric lights 14

Moon 17, 19

night 8, 12, 14, 17, 19,
   20, 22, 26, 29, 30

nocturnal 29

sleeping 29, 30

stars 19

summer 20

Sun 5, 7, 8, 10, 12, 17,
   19, 25

sunrise 10

sunset 12

winter 22

working 25, 26

More Books to Read

Morning, Noon, and Night. Jean Craighead George
   (HarperCollins Juvenile Books)

The Summer Solstice. Ellen Jackson (Millbrook Press)

Why Do We Have Day and Night? Why Do We Have? (series).
   Claire Llewellyn and Anthony Lewis (Barrons Juveniles)